VOLTA

VOLTA

Susan Gillis

George Amabile, Editor

Signature
EDITIONS

Cover design by Terry Gallagher/Doowah Design.
Photograph of Susan Gillis by Terence Byrnes.
Printed and bound in Canada by AGMV Marquis.

We acknowledge the support of The Canada Council for the Arts and the Manitoba Arts Council for our publishing program.

National Library of Canada Cataloguing in Publication

Gillis, Susan
Volta / Susan Gillis.

Poems.
ISBN 0-921833-86-5

I. Title.

PS8563.I5125V64 2002 C811'.54 C2002-904600-9
PR9199.3.G5418V64 2002

Signature Editions, P.O. Box 206, RPO Corydon, Winnipeg, Manitoba, R3M 3S7

for John

Contents

calm; smoke rises
vertically
direction of wind shown
by smoke but not by
wind vanes
wind felt on face; leaves
rustle; wind vane
moves
leaves and small twigs
in constant motion;
wind extends light flag
wind raises dust and
loose paper; small
branches move
small-leaved trees begin
to sway; crested
wavelets form on
inland waters
large branches move;
overhead wires whistle;
umbrellas difficult to
control
whole trees sway;
walking against wind
is difficult
twigs break off trees;
moving cars veer
slight structural damage
occurs; shingles may
blow away
trees uprooted;
considerable structural
damage occurs
widespread damage
occurs
widespread damage
occurs

(Beaufort Scale,
Merriam-Webster's Collegiate Dictionary, 10th Edition)

The House

Before I met you I saw you.
In the way drowned Ceyx was shown to Alcyone
by a Juno tired of hearing petitions for his safety,
I too was given a dream:

mine, of the home I would shortly enter. My mistake
was not one of action but of interpretation;
a woman I took to be your first wife
appeared in the doorway holding a spatula.
Backlit by the sun, underslept, wearing a pink bathrobe,
she offered to make us breakfast.
I turned my face to the crook of your knee
though I knew it had long been over between you.
How small of me to have thought her pathetic.
You were leonine, leaning back on your elbows.
And there was more…

I fed halvah to your children, and they clattered out to the garden.
The whole house—stuccoed half-wall, slate terrace,
herb-beshrubbed hills—I thought I could find it
by following the dream's luscious air.
Because the dream was beautiful
I thought it was true.
I thought I could say "I know"
this and this…

Alcyone's dream showed her the truth about Ceyx.
The dream was sent to shut her up,
and it did, and she grew wings.

Basement Stairs

Sunday mornings my father would raise the bottom tread
like the lid of a piano, my mother humming

a Mozart sonata upstairs, combing my brother's cowlick,
my sisters and I in our dresses lined up on the stairs, our father

on his knees with the shoe polish tins. When he buffed my toe
my whole leg shook. I liked the cloth

but I liked the brushes best, that baffling sense
of being not quite touched, as though my shoes were feeling

for me, the echo of feeling.
Then he would grip my toe.

I thought God lived in that stair, and leaked out
whenever my father lifted the tread, I thought

he followed our car to church
and waited, mute and holy, while my father parked,

and hurried with us across the Grand Parade, the bells
ringing *it's-time-now*, their falling arpeggio. After

the service I'd scuff my toes in gravel,
or leaf mold, or wet grass, without thinking.

Come to that, I'm not sure now
he didn't have a little bench he'd perch on.

Kitchen Floor

These past six days have been equatorial, transplendent.
We eat outside. Tonight it seemed the sun
bugled across the sky, draping Crow Hill
and the Blomidons in satin, rimming the inlets and coves
of Humber Arm with brass and scarlet, gold
at the day's last call and the sly falling in
of the humdrum. Creatures slide away to their night
hideouts and watchtowers; we come in reluctantly,
dragging plates and cutlery and leftover potatoes,
to the fridge grinding on, and on the floor a dark
shock where a wind has come in and blown over
the vase of peonies, the wet petals wine-dark
in the gloam before you turn on the light; weather
gathering over the hills where we'd hoped for stars.

Mallow

In the drugstore parking lot a small frog hunkered,
its skin too dark for health. I stopped
mid-step, both of us
frozen there like first cousins to the geckos,
broke-down country yelping from a truck radio,
a kid's face in the window, bored as plaster—

I'd been supposed to run in to buy bottled water.

The frog turned out to belong to a family
of plastic amphibians recently evicted
from their one-room carrying-case
by this idle little landlord in his idling palanquin
for some inscrutable offence.

When I finally returned you were standing by the car a-whirr.
"Thought you were just going in for one thing."
They were busy? I got your lip balm? Couldn't find the—?

You took the corners a bit too fast.
Nothing looked beautiful yet.
I didn't mention the frog.

Little by little we talked it up, nice woods,
hills to climb, the coves of Humber Arm,
til you reached across the gearshift the other side of Curling
and twined my fingers briefly. The cloud dissolved
and all at once we noticed

mallows in the ditch, *look,* we said,
their pale cups open like satellite dishes
on radio tower stems, catching
signals and signalling.

Backyard Light

We're in the backyard again. This time
we have brought out the gas lantern and lit candles
around our talk. Scott tells of the field behind

a house he stayed in in France, the day he was walking
and missed a step, stumbled over what turned out to be
a Stone Age axe head. For a moment a candle flickered

and dark gathered around the back of my hand
as I cupped the flame. Someone returned from inside,
letting the screen door wheeze. The breeze went down,

and with it the dark, winging the yards, and stars appeared
as small fires across a plain, then flipped
back into place as stars. Our talk

turned to family and how we fly—and how a kid
can't—and somebody's heard—d'you think there'll be—
or will it turn—If hell is repetition....

When we finally fell silent the bats radared out
exactly as if they'd been waiting. Across the yards,
faint sounds of people arguing,

making supper, making love, music,
children playing, and animals.
Did you keep it, I asked him

and he opened the gas, just a notch,
and said yes,
of course.

The Marriage Bed

I won't say I didn't watch her leave.
Boots all the way to her knees.
Hair to her waist.
Striding between the tables
and the dim sum carts.
In her dark lips and
insouciance she looked
like your best friend's daughter.
That is, not yours but anyone's.
Your best friend's daughter,
and here I do mean yours,
has a gravelly voice, albeit musical,
the voice of a much older woman
that erupts from her as though
the woman of the future
exists inside her, impatient
for knowledge and form.
That girl was like that.
After she left the washroom, I went in.
Later at home I thought of her kiss
on the tissue on top of the pile in the bin,
black almost, under the halogen light.
How light deepens the darkness of dark.
The twinning rode with me all night.

Study Window

The scent of lawngrass is filtering through the screen.
Noon is drawing up with its urge toward lunch.
I would like to dip my hands into a well of wet clay
and pull up as it spins, fashion a lithe goblet
and drink your health, and why not
while I'm at it conjure you too, our two mouths
chasing the rim on opposite sides, remembering.
Now the mower has stopped. I hear it cough
and think of the papers pinned to your walls
fluttering on the draught as your lover came in,
and you leaning past me to pour for him. Old friend,
when I left that day I did not know I was leaving.

The Porch

A small breeze shakes the tips of the cedars.
They sway so lightly they skip across sight,
ruffle a place deeper than seeing.
Everything else is very still, day
follows night follows day without moving.
How long now have you and I been apart?
To count with these units seems fruitless.
Sitting with my father on the porch in the dark
watching moths fly up against the screen I said,
Let me put it this way, don't give him any heirlooms,
and the shadow scudded over his face
and out beyond the trees.

Promethean Door in West London

In some parts of the world, doors are painted boldly. This occurs, for example, in the City of London and Westminster, along elegant grey crescent roads.

Where the houses side by side are elegant as bones.

Perhaps you have seen the ashwood door with the small square window centred horizontally two-thirds of the way up, framed with one-eighth-inch strips of ashwood and set behind with a pale panel of doorskin instead of glass, a blue wooden egg balanced on the lower edge?

On a clear day you can see René Magritte standing in front of this door, his back to the road.

His left index finger presses on the bell.

The bell has not been functional for some years now, ever since the butler married the maid and moved to a three-room apartment on the outskirts of the city near the smelters.

Magritte's nose—René's nose—is pressed up close to the egg.

Or so we can imagine, from our vantage point somewhere well back from the door.

But perhaps not so far as the camellia that separates the garden from the road.

Which makes, as this is a Nashian terrace house, for quite a small distance really.

Front gardens here being no larger than handkerchiefs.

The camellia is studded with red blossoms that anticipate their fall even before they have fully bloomed, no sooner open than they brown at the edges and begin their shrivelling.

The door, excuse me, I said ashwood where actually it is painted ashwood. A trick of the brush, strokes become woodgrain, tra-la.

The neighbouring doors are painted oxblood, vermilion, azure, tangerine, aubergine…

They do not have eggs where windows should be.

Then, nor does René Magritte stand before them, perpetually ringing the silent bell.

Nor does a taxi lurch up and spill René Magritte into the pocket garden.

Some of the neighbours are a little annoyed that crowds have begun to gather before the (painted) ashwood door.

One young woman watching the door developed stigmata: a bleeding ear, a pricked band around her forehead, ruptures in her palms. Burning ribs.

It was proposed that the egg be destroyed.

The residents began to protest in whispers among themselves.

A dark wing settled over the spectators' heads, the owl.

Of neighbourly wisdom.

Steam swam around the (ashwood) door, caressing the ankles of René Magritte.

Who stood very still.

You had to admire how still he stood, nose pressed up to that blind little window.

The stigmata healed, but a small, faintly blue bump remained at each site.

Others in the audience noticed curious marks on their wrists, hands, chests.

The neighbourly wisdom pressed from above like a fleet of helicopters.

Journalists began to arrive.

Someone asked what was behind the door.

No one remembered.

All anyone knew was that René Magritte was before the door and if anything was behind anything else, it was the door.

The gardens are full of lilies and the heavy perfume of lilies.

"The Hanging Gardens of Babylon Recreated in a Corner of West London" exclaims the brochure.

A group of Japanese tourists surveys the garden. Tea and cakes are served in the shade. Pictures are taken.

Have you noticed how closely each one holds her camera? Notice how she presses the shutter with grave consideration, then laughing flutters open her face like a handkerchief.

People are wiping their foreheads as they pass.

The owl retreats into the green heart of a horse-chestnut tree.

Summer Holiday

I'd heard chanterelles could be found
near the creekbed on the opposite shore
after a rain so when the air cleared
and the lake was calm we paddled out,

me in the stern for a change, steering.
We crossed under a high circling osprey,
slid up to the bank through reeds
and lily pads; Marilyn stepped out,

hauled the canoe onto sand
bruising the wild mint that spread
in all directions, fur-leaved, stems
nearly purple with vigour. On the lake

the sun had been warm; here
redwood and Douglas fir rose a cool
fifty feet before branching. We started in
through the shade, picking our way

between mud-bound roots toward
the sound of the creek, the ground
sucking at our weight. Marilyn
walked ahead, til the mud

took my foot. Swallowed
my leg up to the knee, pitching me forward,
hands scrabbling at roots,
and I shouted, and Marilyn turned,

but the shout continued on past both Marilyn
and the creek, visible now through the trees,
to a pile of white bones, big ones,
a large animal picked clean,

their light clarifying the murk the way
creekwater sharpens the sound of mud,
the way osprey dive after rain.
Pulling out was a rehearsal for death—

Marilyn offered her arms,
        I held on, we
                pulled. We did,

though she may have forgotten that now.
As I have forgotten
whose arm, mine or hers, sank back
to retrieve my sandal, my

physical memory—strength
of a superhero wresting the hapless
from certain doom—may be invention.
We washed in the creek,

then we examined the bones. Took three
back: a single vertebra
and two longish paddles
with spatulate ends; held them up

to our necks and ears as though
decking ourselves out for a trip to town
and someone took a picture.
Marilyn kept two; the third

stayed on the porch and became
the spine of a wasp's nest.
We did find the chanterelles,
picked some for supper, cooked them

with garlic and mint. I would like sometime
to have another look at those bones.
When I gave her the picture the winter I left,
Marilyn held it by a corner and said "Oh"

and gave a short laugh.
There's nothing mysterious after all;
mud fills a space between roots,
a cow wanders out from the farm over the hill.

Intersection

Leaves were falling, and rain
in strings, nearly straight
down, gravity
doing its jig again, like the
irrepressible men in
the old fishers' home, mated
to the wheeling earth.
Dips in the street collected the rain.
The wet leaves fell
onto the street, wet,
onto the resonant lakes.
The leaves were slow
as duck feathers. I can say
"slow as duck feathers"
whether I've seen
duck feathers falling
or not, because
we are in a blind. Watch now:
a man is about to walk by with a creel
and a woman will cross holding a black umbrella.
They are not related and will not meet,
except in the rain and the leaves.

Love as extended Care

Happy sun, breathing down on the plastic philodendrons.
On the polyester roses. On the flamingoes and model owls

nailed to the trees, on rubber-faced Richard Nixon,
sombreroed and Elvis-jacketed, posed with a ukulele.

On several plaster Bambis, on Snow White gamboling
with the four remaining dwarves among

the red and white spotted toadstools and the tires,
the spinning ducks, their useless wings outspread;

on Raggedy Ann in Farmer John's straw lap, she's
definitely not his daughter; it's

spring, and the Transfer Engineers at the Hartland Dump
are tending their garden next to the tip, dibbing the odd

still-breathing umbrella plant and wounded fern
into their extended-care-ward mixed border, perennial, mock-

mock-heroic—I am driving
over the barrens that stretch past to the north and east.

In the distance a blue flame burns on a high pole.
Somewhere out here is the chipper.

I have flung my winter coat to the ground,
cleared the yard and pruned trees, dragged ramage here

for industrial-scale composting, a transformation
too big to manage at home, and when I climb

back into the truck and shut the door it is true I drive away lighter,
yet I am as heavy with longing as the jasmine is with nectar.

The Sufficiency of Love

For you, I stood on a Cretan hillside kicking at dust
    while the bus was repaired; for you,
I walked gladly across the frozen rivers of Manitoba; for you,
Failed compliantly to comprehend the ancient ways of life in modern Asia;
I crossed boundaries I did not know were boundaries;

I watched the sun cross from this to that edge of the Mediterranean
    on the longest day,
And from this to that end of the northern plain on the shortest,
And saw how its course fails to describe the course of a human life,
    which is not a trajectory;
I have changed my place in the world more than once for you,

Living now monkish, now high, now in torment—
In the steep ravines of Agia Galini, on the low fluvial plain,
Winding coastward down the hills of Argolis under the stars,
Even there I was bound; even free. Wherever, however, I go,

The one constant is my love for you, which is refused. Therefore I say
    life teaches me not
To love you not, but through you, to love.

Love as impending Disaster

Contrary to allegation, love
does not strike from a distance
on diamond arrows, heavens'
multitudes resounding. No, it is
built in: the chambered heart
is a small apartment complex.
It was obvious
when the elevator doors opened
and you stepped out
you were meant to be
my next husband. I'm sure
it registered on my face,
spangling hot and trembling,
though you didn't see it
quite that way, holding up
your briefcase like a shield—
I could have used
a few arrows then.
I paced—below your windows,
as often as possible—for many weeks,
though I knew this was unseemly.
The neighbours began to wonder
and resensitize their alarm systems;
the more experienced among them
started packing up.
I could say I saw reason,
slunk home—but even there
was no peace, that building
is condemned. What can I do
but stand in the lobby
til the final hour?

Love as Stone

That silver thread in the cleft in the hill?
Falling water, like a weighted line.
Plunges down the rockface into the stream.
Up ahead we'll cross it and I'll show you
something of my heart. At the top
the water pools in a kind of stone bowl
worn by eons of swirl, a pool so tranquil
you hardly believe it comes from the same spring.
After the climb I rested there, floating
chin-deep in its chill, looking out
over the caribou fields above the cloud
line, and down, at the string-like road trimming
the shore, the miniscule stream, this bridge
across it like a caught twig—I felt
a warmth kindle in me then, and became
aware of a steady pounding, as though heard
from great distance—the cascade, and
my blood. You have to remember the lull at the edge
becomes a punishing force as it descends,
that shimmer we love veiling the gouge it forms.

The Condition of Love

If love stand behind falling water.
If love were crammed into rock at the world's birth.

If my hands shook as I neared you in the café, sloshing my hot desire.

If to see, to be seen, if seen, my first mistake.
The conjugation is not simple.
If to speak, spoken.

If silence be a useful lie.
If a useful lie be a knife in the heart.

The heart, divided.

If I live in one chamber, you in another.

If a recess in rock be a chamber.

Love shows itself at Night

After dusk's ride-out, small birds
turn in; the doe grazing on alder at the shore
turns back to the forest; night begins
its bristling. I come out to the porch
as the earth tilts northward, revealing
you up there, gossiping with Cassiopeia.
I pace under the stars, shaking my fist
and shouting to high heaven, while you tip back
the flask of celestial liquor, not spilling
a drop, not even a drop, onto my lips
though you know I thirst—And I seek this.

Love's Caution

Cheek like the tulips, form like the cypress,
you have been fitted out to attract
susurrations of longing in festive
rooms from hopeful women with flattering
smiles, and there is no shortage of smiles;
certain it is that among your gifts
is the resilience of evergreens in snow:
do not bend too far, then,
from one who asks of you nothing
more than this.

Love as pure Desire

His skills:

1. whets the knife whipping the blade toward his belt
2. while watching something else
3. usually the people coming and going on the other side of the counter
4. who are coming and going to and from their tables in his restaurant
5. where they hover hushed and reverent over his food

His person:

quick thin and sharp his long torso
dark his eyes which look long at the produce
wide-tipped his fingers which press at cuts of meat
ready his mouth lips poised to taste
in general, all appetite

he feeds from one spring, looking,
looking.

It chanced one day while he was weighing
a small yellow tomato in his hand, his look
landed on me, rippled through and opened my mouth.
"Taste this," he whispered, and eased it in.
My husband one step behind me.
One yellow tomato.
That was all.
But I can say to you, happy is she
who may dine nightly at his table.

Love as an unclear Set of Responsibilities

This building appeared to me from the road. Dark green, it was nearly indistinguishable from the firs. I parked

though I was in no motorcar

and walked toward it down a thin path bony with roots

between which I stepped by angling, louvering my arms for balance. I reached the foundation

and found a wall that rose without windows two stories to a pitched shingle roof. Halfway up was a door but no steps.

I walked to the left and then to the right; branchtips were brushing the walls.

Then I walked around.

Here the forest gave way to a field, charred along the sides, of sweet clover in flower pale and swaying, the earth's epaulettes, rolling down the incline out of sight

and I remembered then that this was the house I lived in. I recognised the screened porch,

the snapping door with its metal catch and spring, the hinge that shrieked when it opened and closed,

and the people inside, who were waiting for me to start the barbecue. They called out eagerly from their webbed folding chairs

when they saw me through the screen. I went to the hearth at the far corner of the concrete patio

and laid kindling and charcoal from the bucket, crumpled paper and pushed it underneath.

My friends and family oohed and ahhed at what I had built.

I could tell they were hungry, and recalled that the food was in my car.

The evening air was warm, and a cool current flowed through it. The sweet clover beckoned in the slanting light.

Three times I struck a match and held it under my little pyre until it caught, and then I walked back around the building and out through the trees.

Love as noble Sufferance

The frost bit-bright, streets
dry as hell's horses' breath, buses
lancing the throughway carrying

everyone, the city
not fit for walking, absurd
trees stopped mid-bud. Inside

my dust-thickened hothouse one-room
I fidget. So what
if every phone call is a telemarketer,

I've long since quit anticipating
the cheer of your voice. Whatever I did
that is so unspeakable

at least the hot and cold of it ran together.
Love brooks all, even
rancour; the quick current

rubbing against ice breaks it up. From this
double lock-up of silence and weather
no word will spring me, nor will spring.

Ideal Love

It's easier to love once a person is dead.
Many people prefer the dead to the living in general.
I know of some who love only the never-living;
snowmen, for example;
but these are the exception.
As for me, there are people
I have only lately come to being able to love.
Death is such a liberating thing.
Think of the famous dead you revere,
could you love them so if they were alive?
Admit it, are you not yourself more alive
(do you not love your life the more)
because you love them wholly, freely?
Why then, living, do you long to be so loved?

Love poses a Question

Once there were answers: things corresponded,
the planets in motion struck
heavenly chords, all was
as it should be. If the humours
got out of sorts, the gods laughed
and fetched healing elements
from the four corners; if Pan, sprung,
made pandemonium, it
was answered. The world
is noisier now, and depleted
of explanations. Who can say
how we are nourished
by land mines or car bombs?
What is a bomb? Tell me,
because my heart trembles.
Brothers and sisters, the earth is a question
that swallows sense. Walking with you
in the Alberta hoodoos, laying a hand
on the bark of a lodgepole pine, letting
the long flowering grasses wash clean
the crowded mind; world-as-it-is.
You asked, I listened;
this much was given.
Mornings, the sun rises
and traffic intensifies for a time;
oceans flood, then recede;
modulations without end.
The world, with you in it; then
kingfishers, rattling over the plain.

Love's Dare

Tsvetaeva wasn't ashamed to write her ugliness
you said. For my part, I lack courage
and though I touched the covers of that book
it did not reveal itself to me
until much later, nearly too late.
On the shelf it was a reproach.
When the time came
I packed up my belongings,
sold a few things, moved away.
Her eyes burn through dark circles
in my mirror. This,
your gift to me.

Love poses as Betrayal

The note said he was sorry about the babysitter.
She was young, he was weak, the usual turns.
Actually, as in most of these stories,
the babysitter is a digression.
There is the wrecking yard behind the house,
there the rope. There is the woman,
unable since birth to clean herself.
There is the knot of their marriage.
Who can say how it came undone?

Love's Bewilderment

Maybe I was rash.
You walked in.

This is the end?
This little puff?

Dürer in the New World: Projection of West Elevation of Di Castri House with Tree

Suppose Dürer had propped behind his perspective window not a woman but a drawing. Suppose he had rendered faithfully the image of a beloved—house, let's say, and set that behind the grid. Watch now—Dürer sections the page, prepares to draw in the lines. The horizon expands. Post for post, gable for gable, tree for tree, he draws. The house, foreshortened, begins to bulge at its foundation. Dürer steps back. Toward the roof the second story narrows—why, this is not what he meant at all; the upper windows are nothing but slits! Vexed, he erases, widens the angles, opens the vertical axis. Adds a low eave over new picture windows. Way in the distance, the vanishing point is flattened beyond recognition. The white birch leans off the page.

Inside the house, a woman sits up, shrugs into her robe.

Sleep Walking

Twigs and scraps of yellow leaf in the eaves.
Outside the window stretching away rooftops and windows.
When the temperature reaches a certain degree.
The dun pigeon ruffles its breast.
I read aloud the blind sheep from *One Fish Two Fish*.
Marching "from there to here, from here to there."
Sam sleeps. I tuck the blanket over his shoulders.

The path is a transverse angle that crosses so.
As I move downward the hill to the left rises.
To the right rooftops and windows fall away glittering.
Through them far below the silver river.
When the air reaches a certain temperature.
Clouds ruffle in from the east dun-grey and bulging.
I pull the jacket over my shoulders.

Driveway

Walking home, the wind not
around but under my feet, ground
level, the evening spent
thriftlessly chit-
chattering with people
I barely know, the cool blowing
snow after the budding-out
spring day instead
of conversation with you,
the street wind-
latticed, hung
with tendrils of wind, the moon
nowhere in the frost-
ventricled night, dark with stars
whose long glimmers frequent
our long-distance telephone
calls, at the entry
to my building the sloped
driveway slick with snow, one
foot then hip shoulder knee skimming
concrete, the wind in sharp
v's like geese veering
over continents below
the racing clouds I used to watch
while I swam on my back,
in a levity that made gravity proud, I

fell, spilling
grocery receipts for
milk and grapes, these
things themselves
already upstairs
in the fridge.

Dürer in the New World: Venetian Outpost/Highway 1

The Italian city of Arco nestles below a hilltop castle near the northern shore of Lake Garda, west of the main route over the Alps north from Verona over the Brenner Pass to Innsbruck.

The Newfoundland city of Corner Brook nestles in a glaciated valley on the southern shore of Humber Arm, below the main route east from Port-aux-Basques across the island to St. John's.

This watercolour was done on Dürer's return journey in 1495 at the expense of a certain degree of truth.

Across the river just past the turnoff for the North Shore Road is a limestone cliff.

The narrow sheer rock could not have been seen from where the view was painted.

Etched into the cliff is the image of a man, his eyes shaded by a peaked cap.

The scowling man looks downwards, his pointed chin particularly prominent.

Most observers cannot tell whether the image was formed during the long Proterozoic or by glacial erosion—that is, whether it predicts or remembers us.

Although initially difficult to spot, once seen it is unmistakeable.

Portrait of the Poet as Tree

Just before I stepped into the tree
Marilyn set up the camera. It was a light day
in the rainforest, light, that is, on a grey scale,
meaning everything shone. All the way up the cedars
to the furrowed sky: emerald, and wet black boughs.
Stand over here, Marilyn said, pointing toward the stump.
She made the tripod stable, and I stepped up.
She frowned toward the light meter.
It's not going to work, she said,
but smile, don't move,
and I obeyed,
and she pressed down.

She shot a roll, then packed up and went home.
She knew better than to raise an alarm.
She has shown the photos all over the world.
Me, now, I host ravens through the light and the dark
and owls come home to my hair.

Dürer in the New World: Corner Brook

The "grand Druid" paces beside the stream, scheming
boulders into the foreground where I want rock,
plain river rock, that's all. I draw
boulders. The Druid, no bigger than a vole,
capers backward into the shrubs, arms
whirring. Puts a white froth on the breakers
—breakers? This is a creek! I'd been planning
ripples, not whitecaps, though I would concede
a daub or two of foam. He's churning up the elements,
it's his fault the creek is pitching
like some Hokusai. Look, I just want
a brook, okay? A burbling mill stream?
(I can talk to The Great like this because I will be dead
long before them.) Well, there's no arguing
with a Druid, this creek floods every spring
and I walk down to it on pine needles
wet from the melt, harking to bird calls and
sap blisters, and when I reach the dip in the path
where it curls up to the bridge, I'll admit
I can catch through the trees
a glimpse of what he means.
It's a matter of perspective
and, of course, approach.
After all, he's not a troll;
I could cross the bridge.

Thanks, Mme Blavatsky

My left leg and my right arm in the back seat.
What symmetry! We drive along imagining
the cop who might stop you for speeding
or running a red, what he would say when he leaned in
to check us out. Whoa! he'd probably say, and,
Step outta the car mister, and get on his radio,
Gotta weirdo here, he'd buzz into the handset
crackling at the end of its coil. You would step out
calmly, placing your left foot on the pavement,
ease your shoulders toward him, you'd stand
and tell him you're just going to take out your sunglasses,
and he would loom, and you would take out your sunglasses
and lower your hands palms forward.
He would check your papers then and say,
So. How about those items in the back seat,
meaning my left thigh and right breast
which you had been thinking about as you drove,
in the context of our last embrace.
Items, you would reply, I don't know as I know
exactly what you mean Sir, since context
had led you to remember
the other parts of my body, that last time,
bringing it all together.
The cop would lean in then, see the usual mess
of newspapers and dog toys
and a pair of rubber boots.
He might have felt then
the strange sense of being watched
but would put it down to some
essential weird vibe of yours, and accuse you
of having tricked him somehow.
When you call me back to you like this
it's hard to let go of a certain lightness.

The At-Home Spider

Once a spider made regular tracks
to my one-room-with-balcony
just spacious enough for us
to spread four legs
to the sun in the afternoons
and sinking evenings. He was
a jovial fellow as far as
I could tell, never
complained, though he drank up
all my juice if I was careless
about leaving it around on counters
—well, counter, since there was
just the one. At times,
and there was no predicting when,
he'd push with all seven legs
—he'd lost one in a tussle I'm sorry to say,
I didn't know my own strength—
til his firm tiny body lifted off the floor
or carpet, or cushion,
and cast a black shadow the size of two sous
in the figure of an eight
where I least expected it.
To the Black Death, I'd toast him
with a glass of scotch
when I could afford it.
I suppose it was August, before the rainy season.
There was a brutish mutt in the yard next door
whose nightly barking dragged me out
with the heaviest garbage I could throw.
Who do I miss more
now I'm without
even a carpet under my back?

Typhoon

Plum branches. All of it—cloud,
rain from the mountains, rivers
overrunning their beds. Video cameras
trained on critical intersections. The city,
ensilvered. Merchants close up their shops,
tighten their collars and head home,
stepping quickly through a scatology of rain,
rivulets in the streets crossed and diverging.
The virile youths in cafés grow still, our hearts warm.
Their faces are obelisks through the streaked panes.
All of us, keyed to the gathering flood,
alert to the first of the fallen blossoms.
Someone reaches for a broom, an arm
leaps in the darkness—the old story-teller
beating the trees again.

Song for the Imperfect

When the moon is a few degrees from full he walks to the river
in a purple robe, carrying his flute.
She is already there on the terrace with her guitar.
He stops in the shadows.
The face of the moon in the river is very nearly the face of the moon.
He lifts his flute, she bows her head, a leaf falls onto the path.

Three hundred and fifty nine times the same song
played before the shy moon.
Over the years he has tuned his playing
to the small constellation of moles behind her left ear.
Never mind, his song begins,
never mind, my sister, you were too young wed.

Crane, I

The robe is purple.
The purple robe covers
trousers, the trousers are white.

The shoes are black, they are not
shoes but black slippers.

Under the robe is soft skin.
Under the robe: no hair!

O he is so young.
He holds the flute
level with the ground.

She is strumming her guitar.
She is facing her mother's house.
Clouds fall away from the moon.

Her bench scrapes on the terrace.
He sees neither moon

nor its reflection in the river;
tonight they are still

so young. So young,
he draws his right foot
out of the slipper,

raises it to his thigh.
On the ground
rest two black slippers

one full, one empty.
Should she turn now, she would see

a confusion of feet! He
is ready for flight.

Accounting

Knees folded beneath her on the mat,
she is as compact as her son's new car,
her spine as supple as the willow she cut
for her own mother's baskets
the spring she turned fifteen.
Then the whole village knew her name
and her beauty was a white bird that travelled
five valleys ahead of her.
So the poets said. Her mother
spoke of her recalcitrance
and her aunts despaired
as though her traits were nestlings
reluctant for flight. Today
she has crossed the province;
tomorrow she will bow before the magistrate
to give her account of her son.
That is something: this son a businessman,
her spine limber as a girl's.

Crane, 2

A single feather
on slate beside the river.
The sky, soaked with stars.

One Gingko

I sat down with you beside the river.
In those days we fancied—but who could imagine
what would come? I sat down with you.
We would walk to the river, you in the lead
holding my hand, past the azaleas and across the lawn,
down stone tile to the terrace.
There were always two chairs.
You pulled yours down the step and set it close
to the shrubs at the bank

and I would tuck in my feet and strum my guitar.
You played your flute—I mean to say you breathed into it
but I think you preferred to watch my bowed head, the moonlight
blueing my hair. You played as though running your notes
through it. Why do I think this?
I am drinking a cup of green tea.
I find it revives me in the middle of the day.
I want to tell you about the view across rooftops from my high window.
Though it is not spectacular, there is a tree.

Cat Speaks, Midnight

Old bowl, you are hard to wash.
Yesterday's porridge encrusts your dark glaze.
Stars prick my tongue, and my paw does not reach
deeper than the Milky Way.

Whistle

The frothing surface of coffee heat-lifted you watch for,
rise to, as to occasion; the mallow leaf as it falls

onto a wooden plate in Fez, air-pillowed, the suras
half-unearthed I hear you sometimes singing

while I brush my hair, the hair I brush
falling back, the train at the harbour, its whistle's

slow pass through fade to away,
a woodthrush, a window, coincident;

the cup you put down beside me, the ordinariness
of putting a cup down beside me before you leave—

9 on the Beaufort Scale

The neighbour's artichokes beat against
the next neighbour's bamboo. I have battened down:
tethered bougainvillea, fastened shutters

but the island finds its way in regardless,
its fine sand, its donkey-brays, dogs and cats, roosters
crying the alarm through cracks around windows

and slats in the door. There will be no more walking
up and down lanes greeting strangers, no more
sobbing, lying half-wrecked in the tub, the stumbling

sigh as water settles around me
the way cloud received the plane on its ascent
frail cousin of a sound you used to draw from me
—I hardly remember—

It slides away, the earth;
its plowed forests, orchards, lanes,
quarries, rock, sand, highrises,
fault lines, magma, veins,
rivers, gulfs, bays, coves,
arms, necks, heads, reaches,
weather—

The Shell

I've heard tell of a creature
thin as a dragonfly wing
said to enter our bodies while we sleep
though how exactly none can say, only
"like a violin motif"   "like my mother's humming"
and it's only after, on a long car trip
or shaking the picnic blanket open onto sand
we fall with a start

into the garden. A kind of grace
perhaps we'd only read about, like that
"after great pain" or "the first startled breath,"
spirals through us then, swift,
yet having once entered, leaves
lodged there a faint beating.

Oh edge-of-my-ear,
what could I have meant, *only*?

This too is widely known

Khalid's wife wears the hejab "not for him, for Allah!"
She is a scholar of the Koran and a feminist.
You say I look "cute" in a headscarf. Well, I wear it
to keep the wind from blowing hair into my teeth
while I chew. Assassin! I'm tired
of listening to your fantasies. Yet your voice
spools out the silky afternoons—
There was nothing wrong in that suburban backyard.
Not with the meal, not with the guests, not with the view.
Rosemary twigs smouldering under the lamb.
A good party, despite sadnesses. A kind family.
Did I tell you, in the village a woman gave me
a bag of apricots, shook my hand, looked into my eyes.
No one asks me in the mosque, Why
do your eyes fill with tears, why do you suffer?
They know my answer is insufficient.
You say the world is quick to condemn; even so
I say *to embrace* means equally *to risk.*

This is not a loss exactly

I buried the cat in the hill I look at every morning over coffee.
Dug the hole, laid it in, tamped the clod over.

It used to purr when you played your tapes of Oum Khalthoum,
Empress, Nightingale, Star of the Nile. You sang along

swirling the offbeats and drones I never could
wrap my tongue around. I spoke like the cat

you said. I couldn't look as I buried it
but now most days I can look at the hill

without thinking of it, and this is not a loss exactly.

But something spins when I look away;
at the edge of hearing, a voice warms up.

I had never tasted such light and fleeting breath

Despola: the name I later misread in Crete
for the smooth-skinned fruit shaped and colored like an apricot

but so other the Turks call it *yeni dunya,* New Worlds,
the spoken words hanging on the afternoon air like filaments

of the old chase after spices and immortality,
Columbus, Vespucci, the others, venturing out, returning

such riches, some are even yet not fully known. This
fruit: cool, a dozen in a plastic bag held out to me

by a woman smiling in a restaurant, if you could call it that,
a few picnic tables and a brick fireplace on the beach,

and a board where the bread is rolled out. She and some friends
were having lunch, as I was. They saw me alone,

as I was, despite company. Strange fruit, New World: when I bit
the essence passed over my tongue and evanesced.

( )

The true story of a piece of fruit:
four pairs of seeds divided by membrane at its core.

It rolls to one side on the table as you name it.
Its bare scent does not linger, even at the peak of ripeness.

Its greeting slips from your tongue before you've understood it.
It disrobes in a market in Montreal

on a flat beside dates
just in on a freighter from Brazil.

The Best Dates in the World, the vendor calls.
Not those, you say. Beside them. He frowns.

Malta plums? You wouldn't like them. Here, a Date,
My Gift to You.... His hand too close to your mouth.

The moment of my arrival all my belongings were lost

Of all towns, that I should lose everything in this
minor hub en route to the coast, place

to set out from, not to settle, Seljuk.
Night approaching, the cold stars suspended.
Rumours of chill northern air coming down.
Histories you wrote for me while I slept—
raiders moving west through the hills above Balkh, your hand
labouring over the jewelled cursive.
Over your hometown the sky phosphoresced.
You knew it was time to leave.
In the dream you woke me, we embarked.
Restless wanderer, if at morning the sea...
You shook open your mat and sang the prayers,
then you vanished from my life.

To sit for hours declining tea in the police station, then finally accepting. The wheels beginning to roll.

The sea has drawn inward

After you left I went looking
as a tourist would, entering your culture
through its city-gates, skirting the popular
destinations, making my way
to the village. I was thirsting
to know what you knew, to say aloud
My love hurts me
to someone of yours,
to scrape out of the hillsides
a place to withdraw to. To leave
only those words, "love" and "hurt"—

I found shoes in rows outside the Seljuk mosque.
I found dogs, and marble toys in the marketplace.
I found women on show as carpet slaves,
their quick hands attractions sold to tourists: all day
the man's refrain, Sit, weave with her! I take picture!
To me he whispered, You do not need hejab
to make carpet.
                    You spoke of fishers;
I saw bank machines in their place. Suleyman,
eyes leaned out from dark backrooms in pharmacies,
whose? That American man, could I trust his warning?

I moved on to the coast to rest.
For weeks, only the sun, the silver hills, heaps of net.
Pleasure seekers in the harbour, their teak deck chairs,
their young cook-companions. The air

stank of preparations: jets rehearsing manoeuvres,
ships nudging the islands. I went for a walk one day
and had to sit down, digging a place among roots.
The heat had taken away my sense; I saw butterflies
swimming, and men swarming through cloud,
the sea in violet clusters, gilded and humming,
flood. All this in an instant

and then it passed. Believe me, I was grateful then
for water, and have not ceased to be.

One thing I should have kept

That small book of Marina's poems
with the pale green cover, her combustible eyes

peering as though from a hospital ward;
it vibrated on my bookshelf

in a way that humiliated me;
I should have closed it up

in a tin or a shoebox, wrapped it in old silk
until I understood why

you insisted I need it;
why should I be thinking of this now

only Henry Surrey's evasions have made me
ready to admit, I have made some mistakes—

I keep a copy of the I Ching in a velvet sleeve
and I do not desire any man, woman or thing

beyond this: a bright window with a long view.
Tell me it isn't impossible.

Gossiping with Cassiopeia

The sonnet is a fourteen-line piñata.

Alas, so all thinges nowe doe holde their peace,
Heaven and earth disturbed in nothing;
The beastes, the ayer, the birdes their song doe cease;
The nightes chare the starres aboute dothe bring.
Calme is the sea, the waves worke lesse and lesse;
So am not I, whom love alas doth wring,
Bringing before my face the great encrease
Of my desires, whereat I wepe and syng
In joye and wo as in a doubtfull ease.
For my swete thoughtes sometyme doe pleasure bring,
But by and by the cause of my disease
Geves me a pang that inwardly dothe sting,
When that I thinke what griefe it is againe
To live and lacke the thing should ridde my paine.

The equilibrium of these lines by Henry Howard, Earl of Surrey fools me into disbelieving the sonnet speaker's claim to inner turmoil. The sonnet describes a preternatural stillness in the world, against which the speaker's overwrought desperation seems melodramatic. The complicated syntax of some of the lines, overlaid with the already slightly unfamiliar early modern English, contributes to this effect.

Surrey's fifteen sonnets, written in the 1540s and, with Wyatt's, the first poems to bring the Italian sonnet form into English, are so hermetic and smooth I want to break them open, to play with their hidden questions, their enticements.

And so I take up the stick, wander into the room.

As many stories do, the sonnets cloak things. What they cloak is often an evasion—a speaker who refuses to be clearly identified, to take a stand, to be held responsible for some action or inaction, despite frequent apparent protests otherwise.

Take, for example, this very odd sonnet:

The fansy which that I have served long,
That hath alway bene enmy to myne ease,
Semed of late to rue upon my wrong

And bad me flye the cause of my misease.
And I forthwith dyd prease out of the throng,
That thought by flight my painfull hart to please
Som other way, till I saw faith more strong.
And to my self I sayd: 'Alas, those dayes
In vayn were spent, to runne the race so long.'
And with that thought I met my guyde, that playn
Out of the way wherin I wandred wrong
Brought me amiddes the hylles in base Bullayn;
Where I am now, as restlesse to remayn,
Against my will, full pleased with my payn.

Emrys Jones groups this with the amatory poems. But who or what is the object of the love? What is the nature of the obligations under consideration, and who is it who doubts and then returns? The urge to rebel, to run the other way, is checked and redirected as impassioned fulfilment of duty, yet the questions hang there, in the belly of the sonnet.

I never saw youe, madam, laye aparte
Your cornet black in colde nor yet in heate
Sythe first ye knew of my desire so greate
Which other fances chased cleane from my harte.
Whiles to my self I did the thought reserve
That so unware did wounde my wofull brest
Pytie I saw within your hart did rest;
But since ye knew I did youe love and serve
Your golden treese was clad away in blacke,
Your smilyng lokes were hid thus evermore,
All that withdrawne that I did crave so sore.
So doth this cornet governe me alacke,
In sommere sonne, in winter breath of frost;
Of your faire eies whereby the light is lost

This sonnet veils its actors and their actions with the language of evasion. "Sythe first ye knew of my desire" and "since ye knew I did youe love" says the speaker, addressing the lady who has veiled herself. So long as explicit knowledge was not ackowledged, the lovers could play at love all they wanted. How did the knowledge come about? Who revealed?

The golden gift that Nature did thee geve
To fasten frendes and fede them at thy wyll
With fourme and favour, taught me to beleve

How thou art made to shew her greatest skill.
Whose hidden vertues are not so unknowen,
But lively domes might gather at the first
Where beauty so her perfect seede hath sowen,
Of other graces folow nedes there must.
Now certesse, Ladie, sins all this is true,
That from above thy giftes are thus elect,
Do not deface them than with fansies newe,
Nor chaunge of mindes let not thy minde infect;
But mercy him thy frende that doth thee serve,
Who seekes alway thy honour to preserve.

The trope of unrequited love is a common one in the history of the sonnet; what's interesting here is the difficulty of describing the nature of the speaker's interest in the lady. Who exactly is it, pleading with the lady in this curious, pristine tone, almost avuncular, delivering cautionary instruction to avoid those base temptations that her beauty will surely attract? Could it be that if he can't have her, then nobody should?

From Tuscan cam my ladies worthi race;
Faire Florence was sometime her auncient seate;
The westorne ile, whose pleasaunt showre doth face
Wylde Chambares cliffes, did geve her lyvely heate.
Fostred she was with mylke of Irishe brest;
Her syer an erle, hir dame of princes bloud;
From tender yeres in Britaine she doth rest,
With a kinges child, where she tastes gostly foode.
Honsdon did furst present her to myn eyen:
Bryght ys her hew, and Geraldine she hight;
Hampton me tawght to wishe her furst for myne,
And Windsor, alas, doth chase me from her sight.
Bewty of kind, her vertues from above;
Happy ys he that may obtaine her love.

Through ease of movement—the lines are smooth, the syntax straightforward—Surrey reveals this compliment to be light and easy, a social gesture, not a serious claim of love. The poet quickly and easily gives space to other suitors, backing the speaker away from any claim on the beloved almost as soon as his declaration of love is made—bowing out, as it were, immediately after bowing.

The primary material for translation is that gesture.

Henry Howard Earl of Surrey was beheaded in 1547 for acts of treason against King Henry VIII. Most accounts depict him as intemperate and proud. His hot response to Edward Seymour's accusations of rebellious sympathies is revealed in his 1537 assault against Seymour in court precincts, which resulted in Surrey's confinement in Windsor Castle as punishment. A night of revelry and carousing ended with Surrey and his friends being detained by police. His military decisions at Boulogne are called into question in some accounts, and closely examined in William A. Sessions's 1999 biography. Late in 1546, Surrey was accused of painting royal insignia he was not entitled to use onto the Howard coat of arms; this was considered a treasonous assertion of entitlement to the throne, and was enough to nail him.

I call it translation, the writing of poems that interpret and represent other, earlier poems, though that stretches the term up to, possibly beyond, the break point, and a better word might be permutation. In writing these fifteen poems, I proceeded as though translating Surrey's sonnets, examining their cultural and historical contexts, linguistic issues, and the spectrum of concerns every translator has to make decisions about—how does the poem's form work, for example, and how should that be reproduced? What are the aural/oral effects, and how should they—or even can they—be reconstituted? What has to be compensated for in terms of image, information, idiom—not to mention cultural connotations? The list of appropriate questions is probably endless. Translation is an inexact art; all writing is, in some sense, translation. It was useful to think of the poem as a kind of ambassador, saying These are ways we thought about things, these are some of the things we thought about.

Cassiopeia, the Ethiopian queen, claimed that her beauty was greater than that of the Nereids. Objecting to this assertion, the Nereids sought and won her punishment. After a complicated series of trials involving the sacrifice of her daughter Andromeda to Poseidon's sea monster (luckily, Andromeda was rescued by Perseus), Cassiopeia was allowed to take her place among the stars in the northern sky, but would have to hang upside down half the night in what Bullfinch calls in the *Mythology* "a lesson of humility."

Versions of her story vary, but they usually include words like boast, vanity, pride, punishment, humiliation...words that dress the real theme of the tale in recognisable clothes. Far beyond simply affronting the Nereids, what Cassiopeia did was this: she stepped out of the bounds of the strict social order, ranking herself, a mere mortal, even if royal, above the higher order of demi-gods.

Surrey was beheaded for much the same kind of offence. In (allegedly) appropriating royal insignia and incorporating it into the Howard family arms, seeming to set himself up as pretender to the throne, Surrey stepped seriously out of line—just what his enemies in Henry VIII's court were looking for, the chargeable offense.

Surrey may have had a reasonable, if remote, claim through family lines on the royal insignia. Cassiopeia may have been more beautiful than the Nereids. Reason and beauty weren't the point.

Some nights at the lake on Quadra Island the stars seemed to jig in the sky as though dancing around living room furniture. I would stand very still on the dock and watch as they twitched. Deer had come down at dusk to nibble on the tender leaves of the lakeshore shrubs; finches were their callers, rimming the lake before vanishing into the woods, abandoning the night sky to invisible predators.

Where better to situate an abandoned lover than in a place this still, yet full of life, indifferent to the presence of human anguish?

The night sky bends our necks back; we bare our throats under its brilliance.

Where better to imagine one who has deserted us than upside down in the northern sky, gossiping with Cassiopeia?

Surrey's sonnet "Alas, so all thinges nowe doe holde their peace," that first one I thought about, plays pre- and post-lapsarian worlds against each other, but this idea has little currency in my time and place. The task is, in part, to create an appropriate corresponding world in which to place the concerns of the original.

All of this presumes, of course, that there is something inside the sonnet-piñata that can spill out and be picked up and examined. I suppose that will have to stand as a reasonably accurate representation of how I experience a poem: however illusory, there are things in it I want to engage with.

In the end, translating Surrey is gossiping with Cassiopeia. She should know a thing or two by now about disruption.

Notes

p. 27 "Love as extended Care" The fifteen poems on love that follow here are radical translations or permutations of the fifteen sonnets written by Henry Howard, Earl of Surrey in the early- to mid-1500s. This poem recasts "The soote season, that bud and blome furth bringes," itself a variation on Petrarch's "Zefiro torno."

p. 28 "The Sufficiency of Love" The source is "Set me wheras the sonne dothe perche the grene," Surrey's translation of Petrarch's "Pommi ove 'l sole" which, notes Jones, is sourced in Horace.

p. 29 "Love as impending Disaster" A permutation of "Love that doth raine and live within my thought," Surrey's translation of Petrarch's "Amor, che nel penser mio vive e regna," also translated by Wyatt as "The longe love, that in my thought doeth harbar."

p. 30 "Love as Stone" "In Cypres springes, wheras dame Venus dwelt" is this poem's source.

p. 31 "The Condition of Love" A companion poem to "Love as Stone," sourced in "I never saw youe, madam, laye aparte."

p. 32 "Love shows itself at Night" The source for this poem, "Alas, so all thinges nowe doe holde their peace," is Surrey's adaptation of Petrarch's "Or che 'l ciel e la terra."

p. 33 "Love's Caution" adapts "The golden gift that Nature did thee geve" and takes its first line from Khayyam's Ruba'iyat:

> *Although I have a handsome face and colour,*
> *Cheek like the tulips, form like the cypress,*
> *It is not clear why the Eternal Painter*
> *Thus tricked me out for the dusty show-booth of earth.*

(*The Ruba'iyat of Omar Khayyam,* translated by Peter Avery and John Heath-Stubbs.)

p. 34 "Love as pure Desire" transposes the gallant compliment made by "From Tuscan cam my ladies worthi race."

p. 35 "Love as an unclear Set of Responsibilities" takes as its point of departure "The fansy which that I have served long."

p. 36 "Love as noble Sufferance" treats some of the subtext of "When Windesor walles sustained my wearied arme."

p. 37 "Ideal Love" improvises on what I have come to think of as Surrey's jazz sonnet, "Dyvers thy death doo dyverslye bemone," in which Surrey both eulogizes Wyatt and criticizes others.

p. 38 "Love poses a Question" translates another eulogy to Wyatt, "In the rude age when science was not so rife."

p. 39 "Love's Dare" plays with yet another tribute to Wyatt, "The great Macedon that out of Perse chasyd."

p. 40 "Love poses as Betrayal" writes a parallel to "Th' Assyryans king, in peas with fowle desyre." This poem is dedicated to Colleen Farrell.

p. 41 "Love's Bewilderment" recasts "Norfolk sprang thee, Lambeth holds thee dead."

p. 42 John A. Di Castri's houses and buildings around Victoria, BC are noteworthy interpretations of West Coast/Modern architectural styles of the 1950s and 1960s. Freda and John Moran House (1955-62), a model for the (wholly imagined) house that appears in this poem, features "free-floating complex gable forms...and floor-to-ceiling plate glass windows" (University of Victoria, Maltwood Art Museum and Gallery: Modern Architecture in BC.)

p. 45 This poem liberally fragments, compresses and misquotes Bailey's discussion of Dürer's painting "Venetian Outpost" (46), and freely improvises on Tourism Newfoundland's descriptions of the Old Man in the Mountain visible off Highway 1 outside of Corner Brook.

p. 47 Erwin Panofsky reports that the 16th-century Giovanni Paolo Lomazzo referred to Dürer as "the 'grand Druid' of art." (11)

p. 59 The line "after great pain or the first startled breath" conflates parts of lines from Emily Dickinson and Jan Zwicky.

p. 62 This poem contains variations on themes and lines from Steve Noyes.

Acknowledgements

Some of the poems included here have appeared, sometimes in slightly different forms, in *The Fiddlehead, Matrix, Delirium Press, Press5 Editions*, and *Vallum*; my thanks to the editors of those publications. I am grateful to the Canada Council for the Arts for a grant that enabled me to complete the book.

Many texts have informed my reading of Surrey and my understanding of the social and cultural history of the period. My primary source for the Surrey texts was Emrys Jones's *Henry Howard Earl of Surrey: Poems* (Oxford, 1964), and when it was important to turn to Surrey's sources in Petrarch, I referred to Robert M. Durling's brilliant and moving translations of the *Rime Sparse* in *Petrarch's Lyric Poems* (Harvard, 1976). W. A. Sessions's engaging biography, *Henry Howard, the Poet Earl of Surrey: A Life* (Oxford, 1999) was indispensible, as was J. J. Scarisbrick's *Henry VIII* (Eyre & Spottiswoode, 1968). Luisa Conti Camaoira's study of Surrey translating Petrarch in "The Treachery of Translation," in *Italy and the English Renaissance* (Edizioni Unicopoli, 1989; editors Sergio Rossi and Diancella Savoia) and Alicia Ostriker's vigorous, insightful "Thomas Wyatt and Henry Surrey: Dissonance and Harmony in Lyric Form" (in *New Literary History,* 1:4) jump-started my own reading of the sonnets. I also consulted *The Translation Studies Reader* (Routledge, 2000), edited by Lawrence Venuti; essays by Gayatri Spivak Chakravorty ("The Politics of Translation") and Jean-Paul Vinay and Jean Darbelnet ("A Methodology for Translation") were particularly useful. Michael R.G. Spiller's *The Development of the Sonnet* (Routledge, 1992) provided essential background on the form. In my research into early modern English, I relied mainly on Jeremy J. Smith's *Essentials of Early English* (Routledge, 1999). Other key texts include Erwin Panofsky's *The Life and Art of Albrecht Dürer* (Princeton, 1955 edition), Martin Bailey's *Dürer* (Phaïdon Press, 1995), and Penguin's 1993 edition of Marina Tsvetaeva's *Selected Poems*, translated by Elaine Feinstein.

Among the many writers, scholars and friends who have been instrumental in shaping the manuscript at various stages and in various ways, I am especially grateful to Stephanie Bolster, Mary di Michele, and Judith Herz, each of whom offered valuable insights and criticism; to Eve Sanders, who got me started on Surrey with a challenge to translate a 16th century sonnet; and to Peter Richardson, Carmine Starnino, Theophilos Vamvakos, Wanda Phillips, Tony Johnstone, and readers/writers in the Monday Night Workshop. George Amabile poked and prodded the poems in the right places and asked useful questions. And as always, I thank John Steffler, for space, tranquility and conversation.

About the Author

Susan Gillis has lived on the Atlantic and Pacific coasts of Canada, and now lives most of the year in Montreal, where she teaches English. Her poems have appeared in many literary journals and anthologies. She is also the author of *Swimming Among the Ruins* (Nuage/Signature 2000) and "Kitchen Floor," a limited-edition broadside illustrated by Lori Doody (Delirium Press,2002). *Volta* is her second book.

AGMV Marquis
MEMBER OF SCABRINI MEDIA
Quebec, Canada
2002